Your Workbook for Self-study CMA

Certified Managemnt Accountant Study RoadMap for CMA Part 1

Preface:

This book designed to get through the curriculum of Institute of Management Accountants (IMA) book, This book in individual effort and not related to the IMA Institute, The auhor developed this workbook to make it easy for everyone to be orineted with all topics and subjuects withing the official IMA book.

The IMA book is divided into sections and topics, and the author categorized theses topics into more sub-topics within one worksheet, so it will be easy to know where this topic related to which section and also the Main topic.

Also it will be easy for you to know the big picture of every topic in an easy way, and get through the details, and will help you also be orgnized when you want to study the whole topics with fast and clear steps.

Who can use:

This book for individuals who want to study the CMA part 1, and also for instructors who deliver trainings on CMA part1 to get organized and cover all the topics.

Workbook Structure:

The structure of this book begin with a MASTER sheet that mention all subjects covered in the book, Master sheets are defined with alphabet (A,B,C,D,E).
Every alphabet include one Section, one Topic and four sub categories.

Note:

You can order this workbook in Excel sheet, by contacting the author.
Author Name: Ahmed Mohamed Rafik
Website: www.ahmedrafik.com
Email: info@ahmedrafik.com

* This page leaves blank

* This page leaves blank

About CMA Certified Managemnt Accountant:

The organization was founded in Buffalo, N.Y., in 1919 as the National Association of Cost Accountants (NACA) to promote knowledge and professionalism among cost accountants and foster a wider understanding of the role of cost accounting in management. Our name was later changed to the National Association of Accountants (NAA). In 1991, the organization name was again changed to the Institute of Management Accountants (IMA), signifying our broader role as the association for accountants and financial professionals working inside organizations, and now we are known by the shorthand—IMA.

About CMA Exam:

The Certified Management Accountant (CMA) credential is the advanced professional certification that delivers tangible value. It demonstrates your command of the critical accounting and financial management skills demanded by today's dynamic businesses, translating into significant career opportunities for you.

Exam Procedures:

When you are ready to take an exam part, please follow these steps:

1. Join IMA if you are not already a member.
2. Pay the Certification Entrance Fee if you have not already done so.
3. File an Exam Registration Form selecting the exam(s) you wish to take and paying the indicated fees.
4. Receive a Registration acknowledgment providing your authorization number(s), testing window(s), and the Instructions for Candidates.
5. Schedule your exam appointment(s) with Prometric.
6. Appear for your scheduled appointment(s) with the required identification documents.

Exam Locations

Exams are administered through the worldwide network of Prometric Testing Centers and are available in accordance with local customs. There are many locations throughout the U.S. and internationally. To locate a Testing Center and to schedule exam appointments, visit www.prometric.com/ICMA.

Exam Windows

Exam parts are offered according to the following schedule:
1. January and February
2. May and June
3. September and October

Exam Retake Policy:

An exam part may be taken only one time in a testing window and no more than three times in a 12-month period (e.g., Part 1 may only be taken once within the January/February testing window). All exam retakes require a new registration along with payment of appropriate fees.

Expiration of Exam Parts:

All CMA candidates have three years to complete the CMA program track. The time period will begin with the date of entry into the program. If the two-part exam is not completed within three years, then credit for the part passed will expire.

IMA Young Professional Award

The IMA Young Professional Award is designed to recognize the finest young professionals with outstanding and creative approaches to problem solving within the accounting and finance profession.

The Award is open to anyone who meets the following criteria:

- Under the age of 33
- Employed in the Accounting and Finance field
- Completed Undergraduate Degree from an accredited school
- Outstanding contribution in a professional role
- CMA designation or candidate desired

To apply please submit the application form, resume, letter of recommendation with contact information, and a response to one of the following personal statements (in 250 words or less).

- Describe how you demonstrate leadership.
- What do you consider to be the greatest challenge facing the accounting profession today?
- Discuss a time you faced an ethical dilemma and how you handled the situation.
- How has certification furthered your career growth?
- How have you positively impacted your company or the accounting profession?

The Young Professional Award subcommittee will select 10 individuals based on evaluation against a set list of criteria. The finalists will be sent to a task force for final selection of up to five winners. Please note, no current member of the Young Professional Committee may receive this award.

Winners will receive:

- Complimentary attendance at IMA's Annual Conference & Exposition and Student Leadership Conference Speaking opportunities at the IMA Student Leadership Conference Discount on an IMA Continuing Education product Announcement via *Strategic Finance*, press release, IMA's electronic newsletters, letter to your manager, IMA's website, and IMA's social media sites.

Source: IMA Website

CMA Study Map - Part 1

A	Planning, Budgeting & Forcasting	1.1	Budgeting Concepts
		1.2	Forcasting Techniques
		1.3	Budgeting Methodologies
		1.4	Annual Profit Plan & Supporting Schedules
		1.5	Top Level Planning & Analysis
B	Performance Management	2.1	Cost & Variance Measures
		2.2	Responsibiliity Centers & Reporting Segments
		2.3	Performance Measures
C	Cost Management	3.1	Mesurement Concepts
		3.2	Costing System
		3.3	Overhead Costing
		3.4	Operational Efficiency
		3.5	Business Process Performance
D	Internal Control	4.1	Risk Assesement ,Controls & Risk Management
		4.2	Internal Auditing
		4.3	System Controls & Security Measures
E	Professional Ethics	5.1	Ethical Consideration for Management Accounting

Prepared By: Ahmed Rafik

Budgeting Concepts

Section	Topic	Sub 1	Sub 2	Sub 3	Sub 4
Planning, Budeting & Forcasting	Budgeting Concepts	Fundamentals	Terminology	Budget	
				Budgeting	
				Budgetary Control	
				Proforma Statement	
			Budget Cycle		
			Reason for Budgeting		
		Operations & Performance Goals			
		Charactristics of Successful Budeting			
		Charactristics of a Successful Budet Process	Budget Period		
			Budget Process		
			Budget Participants		
			Budgeting Steps	Budget Proposal	
				Budget Negotiation	
				Budget Review & Approval	
				Budget Revision	
			Cost Standards	Types of Standards	Authoritative Standard
					Participative Standard
					Ideal Standard
					Reasonably Attainable Standard
					Standered Cost for Direct Material & Labor
				Sources for Standards Setting	Activity Analysis
					Historical Data
					Market Expectation & Strategic Decision
					Benchmarking
		Resource Allocation	Master Budget	Operating Budget	
				Financial Budget	
				Capital Budget	
			Strategy		
			Long Term Planning		
			Short term Objectives		

Return To Master Page

Forcasting Techniques

Section	Topic	Sub 1	Sub 2	Sub 3
Planning, Budeting & Forcasting	Forcasting Techniques	Quantative Method	Data Analysis	
			Model Building	
			Decision Theory	
		Regression Analysis	Simple Linear Regression	R- Squade
				T- Squade
				Standard Error of Estimates (EST)
			Multiple Linear Regression	
			Benefits & Shortcoming	
		Time Series Analysis	Trend	
			Cycles	
			Seasonality	
			Irregular Variations	
			Benefits & Shortcoming	
		Smoothing	Moving Average	
			Weighted Moving Average	
			Exponential Smoothing	
		Learning Curve Analysis	Incremental Unit-Time Learning Model	
			Cumulative Average-Time Learning Model	
			Benefits & Limitation	
		Expected Value		
			Benefits & Limitation	
		Sensitivity Analysis		
			Benefits & Limitation	

Return To Master Page

Budgeting Methodologies

Section	Topic	Sub 1	Sub 2	Sub 3	Sub 4
Planning, Budeting & Forcasting	Budgeting Methodologies	Project Budgeting			
		Activity-Based Budgeting			
		Incremental Budgeting			
		Zero-Based Budgeting			
		Continous(Rolling) Budgeting			
		Flexible Budgeting			

Return To Master Page

Annual Profit Plan & Supporting Schedules

Section	Topic	Sub 1	Sub 2	Sub 3	Sub 4
Planning, Budeting & Forcasting	Annual Profit Plan & Supporting Schedules	Master Budget			
		Operating Budget	Sales Budget		
			Production Budget		
			Direct Material Budget		
			Direct Labor Budget		
			Factory Overhead Budget		
			Cost of Goods Sold Budget		
			Selling & Adminstrating Expense Budget		
			Budgeted (Proforma) Income Statement		
		Financial Budget	Capital Budget		
			Cash Budget	Cash Reciepts	
				Cash Disbursements	
				Cash Deficiency	
				Financing	
			Budgeted (Proforma) Balance Sheet		
			Budgeted (Proforma) Statement of Cash Flows		

Return To Master Page

Top Level Planning & Analysis

Section	Topic	Sub 1	Sub 2	Sub 3	Sub 4
Planning, Budeting & Forcasting	Top Level Planning & Analysis	Proforma Financial Statement & Budget	Creating Proforma Income Statement with percentage of sales Method		
			Creating Proforma Balance Sheet and determine additional funding need		
			Creating Proforma Statement of Cash Flow		
		Assessing Anticipated Performance Using Proforma Financial Statements	Current Ratio		
			Quick Ratio		
			Return on Assets (ROA)		
			Return on Equity (ROE)		
			Gross Profit Margin		
			Operating Profit Margin		
			Net Profit Margin		
			Debt Ratio		
			Time Interest Earned (TIE)		
			Earning Per Share (EPS)		
		Performing Sensivity Analysis	Based on Growth Rate Change		
			Based on COGS Change		

Return To Master Page

Cost & Variance Measures

Section	Topic	Sub 1	Sub 2	Sub 3	Sub 4
Performance Management	Cost & Variance Measures	Comparison of Actual & Planned Results	Favorable & Unfavorable Variance		
		Use of Flexible budgets to Analyze Performance	Charactrestics of Flexible Budget		
			Steps preparing Flexible Budget		
			Flexible Budget Varaince & Sales Volume Variance		
		Management By Exception			
		Use of Standard Cost System			
		Analysis of variation from standard cost expectation	Price & Effeciency variance for Direct labor & Direct Material		
			Effeciency Varaince for Direct Cost		
			Spending & Effecieny Variance for variable & fixed overhead		
			Variable Overhead Accounting		
			Variance for Fixed overhead		
			Using Overhead to solve unkowns		
			Sales Volume, Mix & Quantity Variance		
			Sales Mix Variance		
			Total Quantity Variance		
			Mix & Yeild Variance for Direct Material & Direct Labor		
			Extension of Variance Analyses		

Return To Master Page

Responsibiliity Centers & Reporting Segments

Section	Topic	Sub 1	Sub 2	Sub 3	Sub 4
Performance Management	Responsibiliity Centers & Reporting Segments	Types of Responsibility Centers	Responsibility Accounting		
			Revenue Centers		
			Profit Center		
			Investment Center		
		Contribution & Segement Reporting	Contribution Reporting	Common Cost Allocation	Stand Alone Cost Allocation
			Segment Reporting		Incremental Cost Allocation
		Transfer Pricing Models	Market Price Model		
			Negoiated Price Model		
			Variable Cost Model		
			Full Cost (Absorption) Model		
		Reporting for Organizational Segments	Performance Measuerment Reports		
			Multinational Company Performance Measuerment		

Return To Master Page

Performance Measures

Section	Topic	Sub 1	Sub 2	Sub 3	Sub 4
Performance Management	Performance Measures	Product Profitability Analysis			
		Business unit Profitability Analysis	Contribution Margin		
			Direct / Controlable Profit		
			Income Before Taxes		
			Net Income		
		Customer Profitability Analysis			
		Return On Investment			
		Residual Income			
		RI Vs. ROI			
		Balance Scorecard	Critical Success Factors		
			Effective Use	Cause & Effect Relationship	
				Outcome Measures & Performance Drivers	
				Linke to Financial Measures	
			Non Financial Measres	Customer Measure	Customer Satisfaction
					Market Share
					Customer Acquisition
					Customer Retention
				Internal Business Process Measure	Innovation
					Operation
					Post Sale Service
				Learning & Growth Measure	Employee Skill Set
					Information System Capability
					Empowerment, Motivation
			Implementing Balance Scorecard	Aligning & Focusing Resources on Strategy	Translate the strategy in Operational Terms
					Align the organization to the firm's Strategy
					Make Strategy everybody everyday's job
					Make Strategy a Continual Process
					Mobilize change through executive leadership
		Performance Measures & Reporting Mechanism			

Measurement Concepts

Section	Topic	Sub 1	Sub 2	Sub 3	Sub 4
Cost Management	Measurement Concepts	Cost Beahvior & Cost Object	Relevant Range		
			Variable Cost		
			Fixed Cost	Discretionary Cost	
				Commited Cost	
				Step Cost	
			Total Cost & Mixed Cost		
			Cost Type Relationship	Capacity	
		Cost Drivers	Activity Based Cost Driver		
			Volume Based Cost Driver		
			Structural Cost Driver	Scale	
				Experience Level	
				Technology	
				Capacity	
			Executional Cost Driver	Workforce Involvoment	
				Production Process Design	
				Supplier Relationship	
		Actual, Normal & Standard Costing			
		Absorption (Full) & Variable (Direct) Costing			
		Joint Product & By- Product Costing	Market Based Methods	Sales Value at Split-Off Method	
				Gross Profit Method	
				Net Realizable Value Method	
			Physical Measure Methods		
			Accounting Treatment		

Costing System

Section	Topic	Sub 1	Sub 2	Sub 3	Sub 4
Cost Management	Costing System	Job Order Vs. Process Costing	Job Order	Spoilage	
				Rework	
				Scrap	
			Process Costing	Equivelant Units	
				Beginning Inventory	
				Conversion Cost	
				Process Costing Cost Flows	
				Steps preparing Production Cost Report	
				Production Cost Report Preparation Methods	FIFO Method
					Weighted Average Method
				Production Cost in Multi-Department Company	
				Spoilage in process costing	
				Benefits & Limitation	
		Activity Based Costing	Key Steps in ABC		
			When to use ABC		
			ABC Vs. Traditional Costing		
			Benefits & Limitation		
		Life Cycle Costing	Upstream Cost		
			Manufacturing Cost		
			Downstream Cost		
		Other Costing Methods	Operating Costing		
			Backflush Costing (Just in Time)		

Overhead Costing

Section	Topic	Sub 1	Sub 2	Sub 3	Sub 4
Cost Management	Overhaed Cositng	Fixed & Variable Overhead	Fixed Overhead		
			Variable Overhead		
			Fixed Overhead Cost Allocation Rates		
			Budgeted Variable Overhead Cost Allocation Rates		
		Plant,Wide,Departmental & ABC Overhead Costing	Plant Wide Overhead Rate		
			Departmental Overhead Rate		
			ABC Overhead Costing		
		Allocation of Service Department Cost	Trace Direct costs & Allocate Overhead costs to Departments	Single Rate Cost Allocation Method	
				Contribution Margin Method	
			Allocate Service Department Costs to Production Departments	Direct Method	
				Step Down Method	
				Reciprocal Method	
			Allocate Production Department Costs to Product		

Return To Master Page

Operational Efficiency

Section	Topic	Sub 1	Sub 2	Sub 3	Sub 4
Cost Management	Operational Efficiency	Material Requirement Planning	Benefits of MRP		
		Just in Time Manufacturing	Characterstics of JIT		
			Use of KANBAN in JIT		
			JIT Benefits & Limitation		
		Outsourcing	Benefits & Limitation		
		Theory of Constraints (TOC)	Basic Principles of TOC	Inventory	
				Operational Expenses	
				Throughput Contribution	
				Drum-Buffer-Rope System	
			Steps in TOC	Identify system Constraints	
				Decide how to Exploit the Constraint	
				Subordinate Everything else	
				Elevate the Constraint	
				Go back to Step 1, but beware of inertia.	
			TOC Report		
			TOC & Activity Based Costing		
			TOC & Throughput Costing		
		Capacity Conepts	Theoritical Capacity		
			Practical Capacity		
			Other Theories	Automation / Robots	
				Capacity Management & Analysis	
				Computer Aided Design (CAD)	
				Computer Aided Manufacturing (CAM)	
				Computer Integrated Manufacturing (CIM)	

Return To Master Page

Business Process Performance

Section	Topic	Sub 1	Sub 2	Sub 3	Sub 4
Cost Management	Business Process Performance	Value Chain Analysis	Value Activities		
			Cost Driver		
			Supply Chain		
			Value Chain		
			Value Chain Analysis		
			Steps in Value Chain Analysis	Internal Cost Analysis	
				Internal Diffrentiation Analysis	
				Vertical Linkage Analysis	
		Value Added Conepts & Quality	Internal & External Customers		
			Value Chain Analysis & Quality Performance		
		Process Analysis	Process Charactrestics	Effictivness	
				Efficiency	
				Adaptability	
			Business Process Reengineering	Fundamentals of BPR	Process Orientation
					Ambition
					Rule Breaking
					Creative use of Technology
				BPR Involves Changes are	Fundamental
					Radical
					Dramatic
					Process
		Benchmarking	Benchmarking Process Performance		
			Benchmarking Phases and Activities		
			Benchamarking & Create Competitive Adavantage		
			Strategic Benchmarking		
		Activity Based Management (ABM)	ABM Principles & Process Improvement		
			ABM & Quality Improvement		
			Advantage & Disadvantage of ABM		
		Continous Improvement Concept (KAIZEN)			
		Best Practice Analysis			
		Cost of Quality Analysis	Prevention Cost		
			Appraisal Cost		
			Internal Failure Cost		
			External Failure Cost		

Risk Assessement, Controls & Risk Management

Section	Topic	Sub 1	Sub 2	Sub 3	Sub 4
Internal Control	Risk Assesment, Controls & Risk Management	Risk	Types of Risk	Inherent Risk	
				Control Risk	
				Detection Risk	
			Acceptable Audit Risk	Functions of AAR	Management Integrity
					The number of Financial Statement Users
					The Auditee's Financial Condition
		Design Contorl to Address Risk	Components of COSO	Control Environment	
				Risk Assesment	
				Control Activities	
				Information & Communication	
				Monitoring	
			Effective Control Principles	Control Principle	
				Compatability Principle	
				Flexibility Principle	
				Cost-Benefit Principle	
		Internal Control Structure & Management Philosophy	Control Environment	Board of Directores & Audit Committee	Management Responsibility Under Sarbanes - Oxley 2002
					Auditor Responsibility Under SOX
			Accounting System		
			Control Procedures	Safeguarding of Assets	
				Compliance of Applicable laws & Regulations	
				Accomplishment of Organizational Goals	
				Reliability of financial reporting records	
				Efficiency of Operations	
			Foreign Corrupt Practicies Act		
			Types of Internal Conrtol	Preventive Control	
				Detective Control	
				Corrective Control	
				Directive Control	
				Compensating Control	
			Methods of Internal Control	Organizational Control	
				Operational Control	
				Personal Management Control	Recruitment & Selection of Suitable Personnel
					Orientation, Trainging & Development
					Supervision
					Bonding & Personnel Practicies
				Review Controls or Monitoring Controls	
				Control for Facilities & Equipment	
			Inherent Limitation on Internal Control	Management Override	
				Conflicts of Interest	
			Documenting Control Polices & Procedures		

Return To Master Page

Internal Auditing

Section	Topic	Sub 1	Sub 2	Sub 3	Sub 4
Internal Control	Internal Auditing	Responsibility & Authority of Internal Audit Function	Attribute Standards	Purpose, Authority & Responsibility	
				Independence & Objectivity	
				Proficiency & Due Professional Care	
				Quality Assureance & Improvement Programs	
			Performance Standards	Managing the internal Audit Activity	
				Engagement Planning	
				Performing the Engagement	
				Communicating Results	
				Monitoring progress	
				Resolution of Management's Acceptance of Risk	
			Management of Internal Auditing Department		
			Reporting Audit Result	Types of Recommendation	Make No Changes
					Modify Internal Control Policies
					Add Insureance for Potential Risks
					Adjust the required rate of return
				General & Specific Findings	
				Audit Evidence	Primary Evidence
					Secondary Evidence
					Circumstantial Evidence
					Analytical Evidence
		Types of Audits Conducted by Internal Auditors	Financial Audit		
			Operational Audit		
			Compliance Audit		
		Internal Audit Assistance Provided to Management			

System Controls & Security Measures

Section	Topic	Sub 1	Sub 2	Sub 3	Sub 4	Sub 5
Internal Control	System Controls & Security Measures	General Information Systems Control	Financial Accounting Information System			
			Operating Information System			
			Application Control			
			Risk Associated with Information System			
			Organization Control & Personnel Policies	Segregation of Duties and Functions		
				Vacation Rule		
				Computer Access Control		
			System Developemnt Control	Analysis		
				Design	Prototype	
					Development	
					Quality Assurance	Pilot Testing
						Parallel Testing
				Implementation		
				Maintenance		
		Network, Hardware & Facility Control	Facility & Hardware Control			
			Network Control			
			Data Encryption & Transmition			
			Routing Verification			
			Message Acknowledgement			
			Virus Protection & Firewall			
			Intrusion Detection System			
		Backup & Disaster Recovery Controls	Data Backup Policies & Procedures			
			Disaster Recovery Policies & Procedures			
		Accounting Control	Types of Controls	Batch Totals		
				Control Accounts		
				Voiding / Cancellation		
				Feedback Control		
				Feedforward & Preventive Controls		
			Application & Transaction Controls	Input Control	Batch Control	
					Approval Mechanism	
					Dual Observation	
					Supervisory Procedure	
					Redundant Data Checks	
					Unfound Records Test	Anticipated Checks
						Preformated Screeens
						Interactive Edits
				Processing Control		
				Output Control	Control for Validating Processing Results	
					Control Regulating Distribution of Output	
		Flowcharting to Access Controls				

Ethical Consideration for Management Accounting

Section	Topic	Sub 1	Sub 2	Sub 3	Sub 4
Professional Ethics	Ethical Consideration for Management Accounting	IMA Statement of Ethical Professional Practice	Ethical Behavior for Practitoners of CMA		
			IMA Statement of Ethical	Principles	Honesty
					Fairness
					Objectivity
					Rseponsiblity
				Standards	Competence
					Confidentiality
					Integrity
					Credibility
			Resolution of Ehtical Conflict		
		Practice Ethical Scenario			

Return To Master Page